The Survival Guide For Kids With LD*

*(Learning Differences)

By Gary L. Fisher, Ph.D.
and
Rhoda Woods Cummings, Ed.D.

Edited by Nancy J. Nielsen
Illustrated by Jackie Urbanovic

Library of Congress Cataloging-in-Publication Data

Fisher, Gary L.
    The survival guide for kids with LD*: *learning differences / by Gary L. Fisher and Rhoda Woods Cummings; edited by Nancy J. Nielsen.
        p.   cm.
    Includes bibliographical references.
    Summary: A handbook for kids with learning disabilities. Discusses different types of disorders, programs at school, coping with negative feelings, and making friends. Includes a section for parents and teachers.
    ISBN 0-915793-18-0

    1. Learning disabled children--Education--Handbooks, manuals, etc.--Juvenile literature. [1. Learning disabilities.]
I. Cummings, Rhoda Woods. II. Nielsen, Nancy J. III. Title.
LC4704.5.F57 1990
371.9--dc20   89-37084
                                                                        CIP
                                                                        AC

10 9 8 7 6 5
Printed in the United States of America

Cover and book design by MacLean & Tuminelly
Cover illustration by Lisa Wagner
Supervising editor: Pamela Espeland

Free Spirit Publishing Inc.
400 First Avenue North
Suite 616
Minneapolis, MN 55401
(612) 338-2068

Dedication

For all the kids with LD we've worked with and known,
this book is for you

Contents

Introduction 1

   What Does LD Mean? 2

   What LD Does Not Mean 3

   The Six Great Gripes of Kids With LD 6

Chapter 1:
   Why Do Some People Have LD? 7

Chapter 2:
   Why Is It Hard For Kids
   With LD To Learn? 11

Chapter 3:
   Five Kinds Of LD 17

Chapter 4:
   How LD Got Its Name 23

Chapter 5:
   Getting Into An LD Program 29

Chapter 6:
   You Are Not Retarded! 35

Chapter 7:
   How To Deal With Sad,
   Hurt, Angry Feelings 39

Chapter 8:
   Ten Ways To Get Along
   Better In School 47

Chapter 9:
   What To Do When
   Other Kids Tease You.................................53

Chapter 10:
   Tips For Making
   And Keeping Friends 59

Chapter 11:
   Eight Ways To Get
   Along At Home 63

Chapter 12:
   What Happens When
   You Grow Up?...71

A Happy Ending:
   You Can Be A Winner! 75

Ten More Things You Might
   Want To Know About LD 77

SPECIAL SECTION:
   For Parents And Teachers 83

   Learning Resources
   For Kids With LD......................................85

   Help For Kids With Depression 87

   Organizations 89

   Home And Homework 91

   Bibliography: For Further Reading 92

Index...93

Meet the Authors

Hi! I'm Gary Fisher. I went to college for many years to study LD, and I have written about LD. Most importantly, I have worked with over 1,000 kids with LD. Some of them know me as Dr. Fisher, their school psychologist. For the past six years, I have lived in Truckee, California, and I teach at the University of Nevada in Reno. I help school counselors and school psychologists learn to work with all kinds of children, including kids with LD.

Hello! My name is Rhoda Cummings. I studied special education in college. Now I teach it to students at the University of Nevada in Reno. I used to teach English and Social Studies to seventh graders. I have a 24-year-old son named Carter who has LD. Carter lives in Reno, has his own apartment, drives his own car, and has a full-time job. I have written books for teachers and parents of kids with LD. But this is the first book I have written for *kids* with LD.

Introduction

- Do you have trouble with school work even though you think you are smart?
- Do you try to listen to your teacher, but cannot tune out the other noises in the room?
- Do you have a hard time following directions at school?
- Do you sometimes wake up on school days and wish you could just stay in bed with the covers pulled up over your head?
- Do you wish you had as many friends as the other kids, but you just do not know how to say and do the right things?
- Do you wish your parents would let you do what you want instead of making you spend hours and hours on homework?
- Do you feel different—like you don't know where you fit in?
- Do you feel that you are all alone in the world and that no one really understands you—including yourself?

If you can say YES to any of these questions, then this book is for you.

What Does LD Mean?

What does LD mean? That's a good question. Some people say it means "learning disabled." Others say it means "learning different."

We cannot decide what it means for everyone. But we know what it means for us. When we say LD, we mean "learning different."

Everyone learns in their own way. Some kids learn to read at age four. Others always have a hard time reading. And even kids who are great readers may have problems learning in another area such as math.

A few students have a tough time with all of their school work. But they may be good at other things like playing video games, building models, or working in the yard.

Just because kids with LD have a tough time learning doesn't mean they're dumb. It means they learn differently from other kids.

LD for many people means "learning disabled."
To them, a person with LD is a person
with "learning disabilities."

But to others, LD means "learning different."
To them, a person with LD is a person
with "learning differences."

Gary says: "Once I was testing a seven-year-old boy. He was in the second grade and seemed to be very smart. But the tests showed that he had LD. I tried to explain to him what it means to have LD. After I was finished, the boy just looked at me with tears in his eyes. He said, 'But why can't I learn to read?'"

That's why we wrote this book. We want to answer questions like that one in a way all kids can understand. We also want to help kids who have LD with questions about school, friends, and the future.

But mostly we want to help you know that you are not alone.

What LD Does Not Mean

It may be hard to say what LD means. But everyone agrees on what LD *does not* mean:

- It *does not* mean you are retarded!
- It *does not* mean you are dumb!
- It *does not* mean you are lazy!
- It *does not* mean you will have a low-paying job when you grow up!

Maybe you wish you did not have LD. But don't let LD stop you from becoming the best person you can be.

In fact, you might be surprised to find out that many of your problems will get better once you leave school.

Rhoda says: "My son, Carter, has LD. He has been out of school for a few years now. A while ago I asked him how it felt to have LD. He said, 'I don't know, since I'm not in school anymore.'"

Look for answers in this book to:

1. Why do kids with LD have trouble learning?

2. What can kids with LD do about having LD?

3. Are kids with LD retarded?

4. Why do kids with LD have a hard time in school?

5. Why don't the other kids understand kids with LD?

6. What happens to kids with LD when they grow up?

This book will not clear up all of your problems. But we think it can help you understand yourself better. It can give you some ideas about how to make school better for yourself. And it can help you get ready for the future.

After you finish reading *The Survival Guide For Kids With LD*, you might want to write to us. We would be glad to hear from you. Let us know how our book helped you. Or give us some ideas for making our book even better. You can send your letter to:

Gary Fisher and Rhoda Cummings
c/o Free Spirit Publishing
400 First Avenue North, Suite 616
Minneapolis, MN 55401

Best Wishes,
Gary Fisher and Rhoda Cummings
January 1990

THE SIX GREAT GRIPES
OF KIDS WITH LD

Many kids with LD have told us about their problems. Here are the six things that bother them the most.

1

No one explains what LD is, so we spend a lot of time worrying about what is wrong with us.

2

We feel confused in school about what we are supposed to do.

3

Our parents, teachers, and the other kids are not patient with us most of the time.

4

We do not have many friends.

5

Kids often tease us and we get in trouble.

6

We do not like being called retarded or dumb.

Chapter 1:
Why Do Some People Have LD?

Not all people with LD are the same. Some have only a few problems with learning. Some are great in reading but have lots of trouble with math. Many have problems learning everything from writing to math, reading, and spelling. They might even have trouble learning how to make friends.

Gary says: "Once I worked with a boy named Kelly*. Kelly was a very bright kid with LD. He had a lot of trouble with spelling. But when he got to high school, Kelly was one of the best math students in the whole school."

"Kelly" is not the real name of the student Gary worked with. In this book, we do not use the real names of people we know. We use made-up names instead, to respect their privacy.

Gary says: "Another time, I worked with a girl named Sherry. Sherry was eight years old. She was having trouble learning to add simple numbers, but she could read very well. I found out that Sherry had LD."

No one knows everything about LD. We do not know why there are so many different ways to have LD. And we do not always know why some people have LD when others do not. There may be many different reasons.

Some Reasons For LD

1. *Some kids learn less than other kids before they start school.*

Some kids learn a lot before they ever get to school. Maybe they learn to read, write, and do math when they are only four or five years old.

Other kids do not learn as much before they start school. They are behind from the start. They need to catch up. Catching up can be hard to do.

2. *Some kids have problems with learning from the start.*

Maybe it is hard for them to learn to catch a ball. Or stay in the lines when they color. Or understand the rules of a game. Maybe they have trouble learning to talk. Or they cannot understand what other people are saying.

When these kids start school, things get worse. All of a sudden they are supposed to read, write, and do math. They try to read, write, and do math. But they cannot understand how to do these things. Some of them find it very hard to remember numbers and letters. Holding a pencil and writing is hard, too.

Maybe you remember having some of these problems. Did you feel badly when you could not do as well as the other kids? Were some things hard work for you, when they seemed like fun for other kids?

3. *Sometimes having LD seems to run in families.*

If kids have aunts, uncles, or parents with LD, the kids could have LD, too. But there are many people who seem to be the only ones in their families with LD.

4. *Some kids with LD had problems when they were babies.*

Or even before they were born. Maybe their mother was sick. Or maybe they had a hard time being born. Or maybe they got very sick soon after they were born.

Some people think these things could cause LD. But nobody knows for sure.

So, there seem to be many reasons why some people have LD. Until we learn more about LD, this is the best thing we can say about it: Some kids just have a hard time learning. And nobody knows exactly why.

How Adults Find Out When A Kid Has LD

Students who have a hard time learning sometimes get too far behind. So their teacher asks for help. He or she talks to the LD teacher or the school principal.

Then these kids take some tests (if their parents say it's okay). The tests can help tell if they have LD. If they do, they may start to go to the LD room for some extra help.

It is possible that some of these kids will be able to catch up with the others. Then they will no longer go to LD classes. But most kids with LD will always go to LD classes for help.   They may always have to learn in a different way,

even when they get out of school. Maybe it's because they hear and see things differently from other people.

Do you hear and see things differently from other kids? To find out, ask yourself these questions.

1. When someone tells a joke, do I laugh at the wrong time? Or do I think the joke is not funny?

2. When my teacher gives directions, can I only remember one part of them?

3. When I try to read, do the letters move around on the page?

4. Is it hard to listen to my teacher because I hear other sounds, such as lights buzzing or pencils dropping?

Are you a kid with LD? Why do you think you have LD?

Maybe your problem will go away. Maybe it will not. Read on to find out more.

Chapter 2:

Why Is It Hard For Kids With LD To Learn?

Why is it hard for kids with LD to learn? To help you understand, we will talk about your ears. Then we will talk about your eyes.

How Your Ears Work

Sound travels through the air in sound waves. These waves are like the waves you can see in water. But you cannot see sound waves. You can only hear them.

Your ears are machines that can hear sound waves. The waves go into the ear. The ear has an eardrum and some bones that can change the waves. They change the waves into special signals the brain can understand. Then the sound can travel to the brain.

Let's say a dog barks. The bark travels to your ear in sound waves. The sound waves move through the ear and into the brain. The brain tells you that the sound is a bark.

For some kids with LD, the brain cannot understand what the ears send it. A dog barks, and the sound waves reach the ear. But the brain "hears" something else. Or maybe the brain cannot tell that the sound came from the dog.

Read what R.J. says about having LD:

"I can't hear good. I can't talk good. I can't write good. Sometimes it's hard to figure out the right answer. It's hard to learn."

— R. J., 11

How Your Eyes Work

Your eyes take in whatever you look at. Like your ears, they have a special way of sending what they take in to the brain. It is the brain's job to help you understand what you are seeing.

Let's say you are looking at the word READ. Your eyes see the letters R E A D. If you have good eyes, you can see them clearly. Your eyes send the four letters to your brain. Then your brain must decide that those four letters are the word READ. You might start to think about a kid reading a book.

For some kids with LD, the eyes may see the word READ. But READ never gets to the brain. The kid sees something else instead. Maybe the letters are moving all over the paper. Or the letters are blurred together in a funny way.

Aleisha, one of Rhoda's students with LD, says it was hard for her to read. The letters kept moving up off the paper.

Do you have trouble reading? Maybe it is because your brain cannot give you the right words. Your eyes are okay. They work like everyone else's eyes do. But your brain "sees" the words differently.

Ways To Learn — Even If Your Brain Works Differently

Other problems may happen when a brain works differently.

Some kids with LD have no sense of time. Others do not have good body balance. Some cannot understand what other people want or are feeling. Still others seem to see and hear everything that is going on at once. It is hard for them to pay attention to one thing at a time.

How can you learn if your brain works differently? LD teachers have ways to help. If reading is hard for you, perhaps you can listen to books on tape. If you can read, but you cannot understand what your teachers or parents tell you, then maybe they can write things down for you instead. There are lots of different ways to learn!

If you do not understand what you see or hear, tell your teachers. Ask them to help you think of other ways to learn. Then you can learn things the other kids do. You will just learn them in your own way.

OTHER WAYS TO LEARN

Here are some ideas for other ways to learn. Your teacher can help you think of more.

☞ Ask a friend for help.

☞ Trace new words with your fingers as you read them.

☞ Make a window in a paper strip. Put the window over words as you read them.

☞ Read aloud instead of reading silently.

☞ Build a model or draw a picture instead of writing a report. (But first, ask your teacher if this is okay.)

☞ Ask your teacher to put fewer math problems on a page. Maybe your teacher can put 5 math problems on 4 pages instead of 20 problems on 1 page.

☞ Use toothpicks, pennies, or other objects to practice adding and subtracting numbers.

☞ Write math problems on graph paper to line them up straight.

☞ Learn to use a computer for writing.

REMEMBER: IF YOU NEED HELP, ASK!

Ask your teachers. Ask your parents. Don't keep it a secret.

On pages 85–87 of this book, there is a list of things that can help you learn. Show this list to your teachers and your parents.

Chapter 3:
Five Kinds Of LD

Now you know some things about why some people have LD. And you know some things about why it is hard for kids with LD to learn.

But did you know that there are five different kinds of LD? Reading about these will help you understand more about LD. We will also tell you about some kids we know who have these kinds of LD.

1. School Work LD

Kids with this kind of LD have trouble learning to read, write, or do math. Maybe they can do one of those things well, but not the others. But they are good at things like art, sports, fixing things, or making friends.

Rhoda says: "I once had a student named Jeremy. He was tall and handsome and had a lot of friends, especially girlfriends. He played football and baseball. He was one of the most popular kids in school. His only problem was that he couldn't read. Because he was smart, Jeremy figured out other ways to learn by listening or looking at pictures. Now he has graduated from high school and is a successful salesman."

▼ ━━━━━━━━━━━━━━━━━━━━━━━━━━ ▼

The official name for School Work LD is
"Academic Learning Disability"

(AK ə DEM ik LUR ning DIS ə BIL ə tē)

▲ ━━━━━━━━━━━━━━━━━━━━━━━━━━ ▲

2. Talking And Listening LD

Kids with this kind of LD have good ideas, but they cannot find the right words to tell other people about their ideas.

They can hear other people saying words, but they have a hard time understanding what the words mean. Other people sometimes think they are not listening.

Kids with this kind of LD might ask other people to say things over again. Sometimes those people get angry or laugh at them.

We know a boy with LD whose name is Shawn. One day his history teacher was telling the class about the different kinds of Indian arrowhead points. When she asked the class to name the different kinds of points, Shawn raised his hand. Then he said, "The first one is the decimal point." All the kids in the class laughed. Shawn laughed, too, but he did not know what he had said that was so funny.

▼ ─────────────────────── ▼

The official name for Talking and Listening LD is "Language Learning Disability"

(LANG gwij LUR ning DIS ə BIL ə tē)

▲ ─────────────────────── ▲

3. Paying Attention LD

Some kids have trouble paying attention. They have many ideas in their heads at once. The teacher is talking, but what the teacher says reminds them of something else. They hear other noises in the room, too. They cannot block ideas out of their heads. So they end up thinking about many different ideas at the same time.

Mary Elizabeth is a friend of ours with LD. Once she was riding in Rhoda's car. Three other kids were in the back seat, talking to each other. Mary Elizabeth was in the front seat and was trying to tell Rhoda about her new puppy. Every time she started to tell the story, she would stop and listen to what the kids in the back were saying. She started the story over four times. Finally Rhoda asked the kids in the back seat to stop talking. Then Mary Elizabeth was able to finish her story about the puppy.

▼ ▼

The official name for Paying Attention LD is
"Attention Deficit Disorder"

(ə TEN shen DEF ə sit dis OR dər)

▲ ▲

4. Moving LD

Many kids with LD move slowly. They have trouble holding a pencil or crayon in their hands. Their handwriting is hard to read. Sometimes they get low grades because their work is messy. Some of them are not good at games and sports, and they may be the last ones chosen to be on a team. Other kids might tease them and call them clumsy.

We know a kid with LD named Jermaine who has just learned to write using a computer. He is very excited because he has always gotten low grades for messy papers. His papers often had holes in them because he had to erase so much. Now he can fix his mistakes on the computer! And he can turn in neat, clean papers.

▼ ▼

The official name for Moving LD is
"Motor Disability" or "Perceptual Motor Disability"
(pər SEP choo əl MO tər DIS ə BIL ə tē)

▲ ▲

5. Feelings LD

A few kids with LD have trouble understanding how other people are feeling.

People often show how they feel by what they do. They send "signals" with their bodies, voices, and words. To most people, a frown is a "signal" that someone is unhappy. An angry voice means "Watch out!"

Kids with this kind of LD cannot understand these "signals." They cannot tell how other people are feeling.

Rhoda says: "One time when my son, Carter, was 10 years old, we were standing in line at the grocery store. A very fat woman was standing in front of us. Carter looked at the woman. Then he very loudly asked me if the woman was going to have a baby. I frowned and shook my head 'no.' This meant that I wanted Carter to be quiet. But he did not understand that I meant this. He asked the same question again, only louder!"

▼ ▼
The official name for Feelings LD is
"Social Skills Deficit" or "Social Perceptual Disability"

(sō shəl per SEP choo əl DIS ə BIL ə tē)
▲ ▲

What kind of LD do you think you have?
Do you have more than one kind of LD?

Chapter 4:

How LD Got Its Name

Many years ago, no one ever said, "That person has LD." But even then, some smart kids had trouble learning. Their parents wanted to help. They knew their children were smart and could learn. They wanted teachers and other people to think of ways to help their children.

All over the country, parents began to talk to teachers and school principals. Soon these parents found out about each other and began to work together.

Finally, in 1963, they had one big meeting in Chicago. Parents came to it from all over the country. It was this group of parents that decided to call their kids "LD." And they called themselves the LDA* group.

LDA wanted to tell other people what LD means. They wanted a way to decide who had LD. And they wanted a way to decide who did not have LD. .

It was a hard job. Finally they decided this: "Retarded" and "LD" are not the same. People who are retarded cannot be called "people with LD." People with LD cannot be called "retarded." People with LD are as smart as most other people. They just learn differently.

---

* LDA stands for "Learning Disabilities Association."(Formerly ACLD, INC.) The group is for both children and adults with LD. There may be a local chapter in your area. To find out more about it, write to: LDA, 4156 Library Road, Pittsburgh, PA 15234. Or call (412) 341-1515.

People who are retarded cannot learn many things. People with LD *can* learn many things, even if they must learn them in different ways. Some people with LD are very smart, even gifted!

Did you ever think that *you* were retarded?
Now you know that you are not.
Instead, you have LD.
You have **L**earning **D**ifferences.

This does not mean that school will be easy for you. It means that you *can* learn. How easy or how hard it will be depends on YOU yourself, and on your parents and teachers.

The good news is this: You are as smart as the other kids! You can learn what they can learn!

The trick is to know this: You learn differently. Find a different way. Then you can learn!

How LD Rooms Got Started

A lot happened after the first LDA meeting. Many people heard about LD. Teachers who wanted to help kids with LD wrote about special ways to teach them. And schools formed special classrooms for kids with LD.

Usually, these classes were very small. There would be one teacher and only five or six students in the class. The teacher used the special ways to help kids with LD learn.

Psychologists wrote tests that helped them find out who had LD and who did not. Students whose teachers thought they had LD took the tests. If the psychologist thought a student had LD, then the student would go to an LD classroom.

▼ ━━━━━━━━━━━━━━━━━━━━━━━━━━━━━ ▼

Psychologist (sī KOL ə gist)
means "a person who studies the mind and the way
it works." Psychologists know how to give tests
to see if a student has LD. They can also help
kids with LD find ways to learn things.

▲ ━━━━━━━━━━━━━━━━━━━━━━━━━━━━━ ▲

A Law For Students With Special Needs

Sometimes, though, students were put into LD classes by mistake. Maybe they learned in a different way because they spoke a different language. Or maybe they came from a different race or background. Many people began to wonder if these kids really belonged in LD classes.

Finally some parents went to court. They asked a judge to decide if it was right for kids to be put into LD classes just because they could not speak English, or because they did not make a good score on a test.

The judge listened to the parents. New laws were made to keep kids from being put into LD classes, or other special classes, by mistake.

The most important new law was passed in 1975. This law was called Public Law 94-142.* It was important for many reasons.

- It said that all kids, no matter what kind of problems they have, must be allowed to go to school.
- It said that all kids must be taught in the right kind of classes to help them learn.
- The law also said that no student would be put into a special class just because the student scored low on a test.

What The Law Meant For Students With LD

After Public Law 94-142 was passed, many students with LD were put in regular classrooms. They left their regular classrooms to go to a place called the "resource room." The resource room teacher helped them with the work they did in the regular classroom.

▼ ─────────────────────── ▼

Resource room (R͞E sors r͞o͞om)
means "a room where students with special needs go for part of the day to get special help with their school work."

▲ ─────────────────────── ▲

Many people thought this was a better idea. They thought kids with LD would like being in class with kids who did not have LD. Moving kids with LD into the regular classroom was called "mainstreaming."

Public Law 94–142 is also called "The Education For All Handicapped Children Act of 1975."

Mainstreaming was good for many kids with LD. They got to be in a regular classroom, and they got help in the resource room. However, mainstreaming was not good for ALL kids with LD. Some kids needed small classrooms. They needed to have special ways to learn reading, math, and writing all day long.

Tran's Story

Tran is 10 years old. He goes to a resource room for one hour a day. He has a lot of friends who do not have LD. He has some trouble with reading, but he is good at math, and he likes to play soccer. His resource room teacher helps him with his reading.

Kendra's Story

Kendra is the same age as Tran. When she talks, it is hard to understand her. She has trouble with all of her school work. When she was in a regular classroom, the kids sometimes teased her. They said things like, "You talk funny!"

Because she needs more help in school than Tran does, Kendra goes to a special classroom all day long. She gets special help with all her school work. With good help, maybe someday she will go to some classes in a regular classroom.

An LD teacher does more than just help kids with school work. An LD teacher helps students listen and talk better, write better, even make friends easier. As kids with LD learn to do these things, they can start spending less time with the LD teacher and more time in a regular classroom.

For many kids with LD, the LD room is a place where it is quieter and easier to pay attention. It is a place where it is always okay to have learning differences.

Chapter 5:
Getting Into An LD Program

Public Law 94-142 said that *all* kids, no matter what kind of problems they have, must be allowed to go to school. It said that *all* kids must be taught in the right kind of classes to help them learn.

This meant kids with LD, too. The parents in the LDA group made sure that the law did not leave their children out.

Kids with LD are not the only ones with special needs. In fact, Public Law 94-142 talks about four kinds of kids with special needs. All four kinds get help. But more kids with LD go to special classes. Why? Because there are more kids with LD than kids with other special needs.

Four Kinds Of Kids With Special Needs

1. *Emotionally Disturbed* (i MŌ shə nl ə dis TURBD) means "having problems with the way one acts or feels."

   All kids have some problems with things like getting along at school or daydreaming. But kids who have these problems all the time need special help. Kids who are emotionally disturbed were either born that way, or they come from families that have problems.

2. *Retarded* (ri TAR did)

means "slow to learn and not able to learn many things."

3. *Learning Disabled* (LD) (dis Ā bəld)

means "having problems with learning and needing to learn things in a different way, even though being as smart as the other kids."

4. *Physically or Sensory Handicapped*

(FĪZ i klē or SEN sə rē HAN dē kapt)

means "having a problem like being in a wheelchair or being blind or deaf."

All kids with special needs are called "handicapped" by Public Law 94-142. This includes kids who are emotionally disturbed, retarded, or have LD.

How The Law Works

The law tells your school how to decide who has LD and who can be in LD classes. For each student with LD, it may happen a little differently.

Bill's Story

When Bill was nine years old, his mom took him to the doctor because he was having stomachaches. The doctor couldn't find anything wrong with Bill. So he asked Bill if anything was wrong at school or home.

When Bill said he didn't like school, the doctor asked him some questions about school work. He talked to Bill's mom about what Bill was like when he was younger.

The doctor thought Bill might have LD. So he had Bill's mom tell the school principal to have Bill tested. The doctor called the principal, too! Bill was tested. The tests showed that Bill had LD. After Bill began to get help from the LD teacher, the stomachaches went away.

Sandy's Story

When Sandy was 10 years old, her dad read a story in a magazine about LD. He thought Sandy sounded like the kids in the story. He called Sandy's teacher to ask how he could find out if Sandy had LD. The teacher thought that Sandy was just "slow." But the teacher made sure Sandy got tested. It turned out that Sandy did have LD. So she got the reading help she needed in the resource room.

How Did You Get Into An LD Program?

You read Bill's story and Sandy's story. Different kids get into LD programs in different ways, and for different reasons.

How did *you* get into an LD program? Maybe your story goes something like this.

First, your teacher may have noticed that you were having a problem with learning. She (or he, if your teacher is a man) sent a note home to your parents. The note asked if some other people at your school could meet you and try to help.

If it was okay with your parents, then you probably were taken into another room and given some tests.

Do you remember the tests? Perhaps you made shapes with blocks or copied shapes from cards. Maybe you repeated numbers or put pictures in order to tell a story. You also took tests in reading, spelling, and math.

The person who gave you these tests may have been a psychologist. Another person probably tested your ears to see if you could hear, and your eyes to see if you could see. Someone else may have come into your class to watch you for a while to see how you follow directions, pay attention, and do your work. You may not have known that person was even there.

After these things were done, your teacher, and the people who tested you, got together to decide if you should go to LD classes.

The law says that you cannot go to LD classes if you are retarded. You cannot go to LD classes if you are emotionally disturbed, have a problem with your eyes or ears, or have not had a chance to learn. Before you can go to LD classes, the tests must show that you are able to learn even though you are not learning.

If your teacher and the people who tested you thought you should have some special help, they met with you and your parents in an IEP meeting. The reason for this meeting was to decide what you should learn and how you would be taught it. Together they came up with a special plan that was just right for you. Then, if it was okay with your parents, you started going to LD classes.

▼ ━━━━━━━━━━━━━━━━━━━━━━━━ ▼

IEP means "Individualized Education Program."

(in də VIJ ōō ə LĪZD   EJ ōō KĀ shən PRŌ gram)

This is a plan for one kid that tells what that kid will learn that year and how he or she will learn it.

▲ ━━━━━━━━━━━━━━━━━━━━━━━━ ▲

An IEP meeting is held each year for every student in LD classes. Every three years, each student with LD must be tested again to see if he or she should still be in LD classes.

Maybe you did not think you were lucky when you were put in an LD class. But many kids have problems with learning and are not allowed to go to LD classes. So, in a way, you *are* lucky. You can get the right kind of help, so you can learn as much as possible.

Read what Joe says about his LD class:

"The LD room gives me more help than the other class. That's why I go. The other kids don't mess with me when I go."

— *Joe, 10*

Chapter 6:
You Are Not Retarded!

Maybe other kids call you a "retard" because you go to an LD class. Some kids are just plain mean. They want to make you feel badly. They'll tease anybody they can.

You may have met some people who are retarded. Many of them are fine people, and they learn to do many things. Yet you can see that they are different from you.

Read what Laura does when other kids tease her:

"Sometimes kids say you're retarded because you go to LD class. I say 'forget you' or I just ignore them."

— *Laura, 12*

Teasing from other kids may remind you that you have trouble with learning. Perhaps sometimes you even wonder if you are retarded.

If you wonder about this, here are some questions you can ask yourself. They will help you see the ways that you are different from people who are retarded.

How Smart Are You?

Remember, you must be as smart as most other kids in order to be in an LD class. Some kids with LD are even smarter than most people, and they may go to both LD and gifted classes.

You can learn what the other kids learn. It's just that you learn differently.

How Much Can You Learn?

If you are a kid with LD, you probably have "learning ups and downs."

Some days it is hard to learn something new, such as how to multiply numbers. You might try and try, but you still have trouble catching on. Then one day, all of a sudden, you understand! You do ten math problems and YOU GET THEM ALL RIGHT!

Kids who are retarded have trouble learning new things, too. But kids who are retarded learn *everything* more slowly than other kids. Kids with LD may learn some school subjects slowly. They may learn other things just as well as, or even better than other kids.

What Classroom Are You In?

Most kids with LD spend most of their time in a regular classroom. They learn the same things the other kids learn. They just go to the LD room, or the resource room, for extra help.

Kids who are retarded usually have their own classrooms. They do not learn the same things that students in the regular rooms learn. They might join regular classes, though, for such things as art, music, or gym.

How Will You Do When You Get Out Of School?

Most kids with LD have a hard time in school. But with good help, most of them finish school, find jobs, get married, and have children. Some of them even go to college. In other words, most kids with LD can grow up and be independent.

▼ ──────────────────────────────── ▼

Independent (in di PEN dant)
means "able to live on one's own
and take care of oneself."

▲ ──────────────────────────────── ▲

Many people who are retarded have trouble being independent. With special help, some of them are able to live on their own, and a few even get married.

But many people who are retarded cannot live on their own, even as adults. Some adults who are retarded live with their parents. Others live in group homes.

Are You Able To Learn?

A person who is retarded learns everything slowly. And there are some things that person cannot learn at all.

Even though it is hard for you to learn, you are able to learn. You just learn differently. Some things you learn slowly, and other things you learn quickly. But you can learn almost anything!

So you see, there are many differences between kids with LD and kids who are retarded. You are *not* retarded!

Chapter 7:

How To Deal With Sad, Hurt, Angry Feelings

Gary says: "Some time ago, the parents of a boy named Luis came to see me. They said that Luis, who was eight years old, was afraid to go to school. Every morning he cried and would not get on the school bus. His mom had to put Luis in the car and take him to school.

"At school, Luis cried quietly at his desk. His mom, dad, and teacher said that he had a lot of friends and was a good baseball player. Luis couldn't tell anyone why he didn't want to go to school.

"I talked to Luis each week for two months. Luis began to go to school without crying. Still, Luis was not happy. But he could not tell me why he did not want to be at school.

"Finally I decided to test Luis, since he seemed to be having some trouble in reading. I found out that Luis had LD.

"Well, Luis got the help he needed in school. I kept working with Luis to help him talk about his feelings and to feel better about himself.

"With special help in school and the chance to talk about his feelings, Luis was much happier in school. In fact, his mother told me that he looked forward to each day!"

Why Kids With LD Have These Feelings

Many kids with LD become unhappy. They do not think they are learning fast enough. Some of them have trouble getting along at school. Or they have trouble sitting still. Other kids laugh at the things they do and say. Then the kids with LD feel sad, hurt, and angry.

Read what these kids say:

"I don't like being LD. It makes me mad. I don't like how I talk."
— *John, 11*

"I talk slow. The kids beat me up."
— *Chris, 11*

"Kids are mean to me. They call me names like 'stupid.' My brothers tease me all the time because of the way I talk. I get mad because I have a problem. I don't like it. I wish I was like other kids."

— *R.J., 11*

When kids feel sad, hurt, and angry, they sometimes cry and say they don't want to go to school, like Luis. Or they might make themselves sick. Some kids get mad at their parents, teachers, brothers, sisters, or other kids. Others get in trouble or stop trying to do their school work.

Sometimes it seems that no one understands or cares what is happening. The other kids do not understand. Teachers do not understand. Parents do not understand.

Often, kids with LD do not understand why they feel sad, hurt, and angry. The teacher or a parent says, "Why did you throw that book?" The kid with LD says, "I don't know." He or she is telling the truth. It is hard for kids to explain why they feel the way they do.

When kids cannot tell someone about their sad, hurt, and angry feelings, the feelings do not go away. (This is true for everyone, not just kids.) So the kids just keep feeling sad, hurt, and angry. It is hard for them to have fun. It is hard for them to do their school work. It is hard for them to think about anything besides their feelings. We call this "feeling depressed."

▼ ━━━━━━━━━━━━━━━━━━━━━━━━━━━━ ▼

Depressed (di PREST)
means "feeling sad all the time."

▲ ━━━━━━━━━━━━━━━━━━━━━━━━━━━━ ▲

Six Ways To Help Yourself Feel Better

Do you ever feel depressed? Here are six things you can do to help yourself feel better.

1. Have a chat with a counselor.

▼ ─────────────────────────── ▼

Counselor (**KOUN** səl ər)
means "someone who helps people by listening and giving advice."

▲ ─────────────────────────── ▲

Many schools have counselors who are trained to help kids who feel depressed. Other counselors may work in offices near where you live.

Tell your parents that you would like to talk to a counselor. Your teacher or principal may be able to give you some names of counselors. Or your family doctor can help you find a counselor.

Even if you are not sure what to say, counselors can often help you talk. You may need to see a counselor a number of times before you start to feel better.

2. Draw your feelings.

If you have trouble talking about how you feel, try drawing pictures that show how you feel. For many kids with LD, this is easier than talking. You can show your pictures to a counselor or another adult you trust.

3. Make a book about yourself.

You can write a book about yourself. Or you can draw a book about yourself. Or you can make a book with both writing and drawing in it.

Your book can have these parts:

Chapter 1: Things I Like Best About Myself

Chapter 2: Things I Would Like To Change About Myself

Chapter 3: Things That Make Me Feel Happy

Chapter 4: Things That Make Me Feel Sad, Hurt,
Or Angry

Chapter 5: How I Want To Be In 10 Years

4. Do some "I like me" exercises.

If you exercise your arms, your arm muscles get bigger. If you exercise the "I like me" part of your brain, it will get stronger.

Here are some "I like me" exercises you can try.

- *In the morning:*
— Look in the mirror and find five things you like about yourself. Say each thing out loud: "I like my _____."
— Think of five ways you would like to do better. Say them out loud, too.

- *At night:*
— Look in the mirror and tell yourself how well you did that day. Say: "Today I did better at_____."

Do these exercises each morning and each night until you feel better. If you like them, keep doing them.

5. Take life one day at a time.

Do you sometimes think that you will NEVER get out of school? Do you worry about high school? Do you wonder if you will ever be independent?

Worrying does not help. Try not to worry about the future. Instead, promise yourself every morning that you will do your best TODAY.

6. Be patient.

When you are upset and want to give up, think about this: Many people with LD did not give up. You can read about some of them on the next page.

Remember that you will not be in school forever. Remember that most of your teachers care about you and want you to learn. Most parents love their kids and want to help, too.

But most of all, remember that you are special. No one else is like you. Look inside and see all the good things. Do not take yourself too seriously. Learn to laugh at yourself. Be patient!

On pages 87-92 of this book, there is a list of things that can help other people help *you* feel better. Show this list to your teachers and your parents.

PEOPLE WITH LD
WHO DID NOT GIVE UP

Nelson Rockefeller
He became Vice President of the United States
and governor of New York.
He had a severe reading problem.

Thomas Edison
He was an American inventor.
People thought he was retarded.

Ann Bancroft
She was held back in school because she had
trouble learning how to read. She was the first
woman to reach the North Pole. She traveled with
the Will Steger expedition in 1986.

Woodrow Wilson
He became President of the United States.
He did not learn to read until he was 11 years old.

Susan Hampshire
School was especially hard for her because she
had trouble paying attention.
She has won three Emmy Awards for acting on TV.

Albert Einstein
He was a math genius.
He had trouble with arithmetic in school.

Bruce Jenner
He became an Olympic gold medal winner.
He had severe reading problems in school.

Greg Louganis
He also became an Olympic gold medal winner.
He had speech and reading problems in school.

Chapter 8:

Ten Ways To Get Along Better In School

A lot of kids with LD do not like school. After all, it is not fun to have problems learning, especially when most of the other kids are not having problems. That may be why so many kids with LD get into trouble at school.

Read what these kids say about school:

"Well, one thing I know is you shouldn't daydream. When you daydream, it's kind of like being in love. You just sit there. If you do that, you won't learn too much."
— *LeDale, 9*

"Sometimes I try to be real funny in class, but the teacher still frowns."
— *Damien, 9*

"When I'm in trouble, I sit in the corner and read my palms."
— *Rob, 10*

There are some kids with LD who *do* like school. Maybe they do not like it all of the time, but they like it some of the time.

If you do not like school, you can do something about it. There are ways to get along better in school. Here are 10 ways for you to try.

1. When Things Are Tough, Have A Chat

Often, kids with LD do not share their feelings with others. They feel sad, hurt, and angry, but they keep these feelings bottled up inside of them.

It is hard to keep feelings bottled up. Sooner or later, the feelings come out. Sometimes they come out in strange ways. Some students with LD stop doing their school work. Or they throw things, get into fights, or talk back to teachers. They get into trouble, and they feel even worse.

When you are feeling sad, hurt, and angry, why not find someone to talk to? How about a school counselor, teacher, janitor, aide, bus driver, or friend? Pick someone you like, someone who will understand. Then go and talk to that person.

2. Keep Your Head Up!

Being a person with LD is nothing to be ashamed of. If someone asks you why you go to LD classes, tell them (if you feel like it). Look them in the eye and say, "I have a learning disability." Or say, "I learn differently. The LD classes help me learn."

48

Believe and act like you are important. The more you do this, the more other people will treat you like an important person.

3. Become An Expert

An expert is someone who is the best at something. Kids with LD can become experts, just like anyone else.

Think of some things that kids your age are interested in. What about collecting baseball cards? Listening to rock groups? Building models? Pick something you like that other students in your class like, too. Then find out as much as you can about it. Ask your teacher and Mom and Dad to help you.

This is a good way to show that kids with LD can be smart. It is also a good way to get attention. When you are an expert, other people will ask you for help.

4. Take Part In School Activities

School is more fun when you do other things than just school work. Take part in school activities like plays, clubs, or sports. Offer to help plan school activities. Let your teachers know that you want to help.

5. Learn More About LD

Find out as much as you can about your kind of LD and the ways you learn. When you have teachers who do not understand LD, you can tell them about it. This will help them plan for you.

On pages 77–82 of this book, there is a part called "Ten More Things You Might Want To Know About LD." Read this part. Then show it to your parents and teachers.

6. Make Friends

Sometimes kids with LD make friends only with each other. It is good to have friends who have LD. But it is better to have friends who have LD, AND friends who do not have LD.

In Chapter 10 of this book, we will tell you some ways to make both kinds of friends. If you want to read about these now, turn to pages 60–61.

7. Be A Helper

Many kids with LD feel like they are always asking for help. It seems like they are the only ones who ask for help.

You can be a helper, too! Maybe you can help younger kids who are learning things you already know. Or you can help another student in your class with something you are good at. If you know you can help, tell someone! Offer to help.

8. Stay Out Of Trouble

For many kids with LD, school work is hard and boring. So they join in when other kids start fooling around. (After all, fooling around is more fun than working!)

This kind of joining in is not a good idea. It gets teachers and parents upset.

If you see other kids fooling around, just ignore them. Keep doing your school work. Then you will stay out of trouble.

9. Know How To Relax And Cool Off

Think of the last time you were working on something very hard that you did not understand. Maybe you got upset and angry.

What did you do next? Did you pretend to keep working when you were really not working? Did you yell? Throw your work on the floor? Quit? Cry? Go home?

These things will not help you get along better in school. You need to come up with other things to do instead.

Maybe you can raise your hand and ask your teacher for help. But what if your teacher is busy? Then you need to help yourself.

Here are two ways you can help yourself:

- Close your eyes, take three deep breaths, and count to ten very slowly and quietly. OR...
- Say "Relax" to yourself five times very slowly and quietly.

When you start to feel better, try doing your work again.

Gary says: "I am not good at putting things together. It always makes me feel nervous and dumb. But sometimes I have to do it.

"Last summer, I bought an outdoor grill that was supposed to take two hours to put together. It took me TWO DAYS!

"I used to try to put things together when I was a kid. I would get so mad that I would throw things and yell. That didn't work very well.

"Now I read each step of the directions a couple of times. I also look at the pictures very carefully. And I work very slowly. I set short goals, things I know I can do, like putting the legs on the grill. After I meet a goal, I give myself a short break for a reward.

"If I get too frustrated, I stop working for a while. Then I take some deep breaths and read the instructions again.

"I'm still not very good at putting things together. But I have gotten better. And I don't get so angry anymore."

10. Do Not Use LD As An Excuse!

Some kids use LD as an excuse for not doing their work.

Maybe a kid has science homework to do. But there is a movie on TV he wants to watch. So he watches the movie instead. The next day, he tells his teacher, "I forgot to do my homework because I have LD."

Or maybe another kid has a math lesson to do. But she does not want to do the lesson. So she tells her teacher, "I am no good at math because I have LD."

Or another kid has a spelling test coming up. He does not want to study for the test. He wants to play outside instead. So he tells his teacher, "Spelling tests upset me because I have LD."

NEVER use LD as an excuse for not doing your work! It is your teacher's job to find the best ways to teach you. It is your job to work as hard as you can.

Even with the best teachers and the best books, some things will be hard for you. But NEVER use LD as an excuse for not trying.

Chapter 9:

What To Do When Other Kids Tease You

It is not right, but kids tease each other all the time. They tease anyone who dresses, talks, looks, or acts differently from them. Probably everyone gets teased at some time.

Gary says: "I was good in school, but I got teased because I have a big nose."

Rhoda says: "For a long time, I was mad at my parents because they named me 'Rhoda Beth.' The kids used to tease me and call me ROTO-ROOTER. As soon as I graduated from high school, I changed my name from 'Rhoda Beth' to just 'Rhoda.'"

Why Kids Tease

There seem to be three main reasons why kids tease. Here are the reasons:

1. They see other kids doing it, and they want to be a part of the group.
2. They have been teased, and they are trying to hurt someone else the way they were hurt.
3. They think that if they make someone else feel bad, they will feel better. (This is not true!)

Why You Get Teased

Because you have LD, you are different from other kids. Remember that kids tease anyone who dresses, talks, looks, or acts differently from them. Because you are different, kids probably tease you. Maybe you even get teased a lot.

- Maybe you get teased about going to LD classes. ("There's the kid in the dummy class!")
- Maybe kids call you names. ("Stupid!" "Retard!")
- Maybe some kids let you know that they do harder school work than you do. ("You're only reading Book Two? I finished that book last year.")
- Maybe you get teased about the kind of school work you do. ("That's baby work!" "You're the worst reader in our class!")

No matter how other kids tease you, you feel sad, hurt, and angry. Being teased is no fun.

The good news is, you *can* do something about teasing. There are ways you can act and things you can say when other kids tease you. Some of these are not so helpful. Some are kind of helpful. And some are very helpful.

We will tell you about all three kinds. When you read about them, ask yourself, "Which ones do I do?"

Not So Helpful Things To Do When You Get Teased

WHAT YOU CAN DO	**WHAT MIGHT HAPPEN**
Start a fight.	You might get beat up.
	If you win the fight, you might feel better for a while. You could also get in trouble for fighting.
	If you win the fight, that kid might stop teasing you. But then someone else, maybe bigger and stronger, could start teasing you.
Tease back.	The kid teasing you might be a lot better at it than you are. Then you will feel even worse.
	The kid might tease you again because you teased back the first time.
Cry and run away.	Now the kid knows that teasing really bothers you. He or she might keep it up.
	You might feel bad about not standing up for yourself.

Kind Of Helpful Things To Do
When You Get Teased

WHAT YOU CAN DO

Ignore the teasing.

WHAT MIGHT HAPPEN

Soon the teasing may stop. However, some kids can keep it up for a long time. They may try harder if they see you are trying to ignore them.

Smile and say it does not bother you.

This is a lot like ignoring. It is hard to do. It is also not good to hide your feelings.

Very Helpful Things To Do
When You Get Teased

WHAT YOU CAN DO

Stand up straight and look the kid in the eye. Say in a calm voice, "I do not like to be talked to that way." Then walk away.

WHAT MIGHT HAPPEN

Even if the teasing does not stop, you will feel good about standing up for yourself. And you will not get in trouble for fighting.

The kid teasing you may see that he or she cannot make you cry or get angry. The kid may give up trying.

You may have to repeat this many times before the kid "gets it." But that is still better than fighting or hiding your feelings.

Talk to an adult you like and trust. Pick a person who is a good listener and who cares about you. Tell that person about the teasing and how you feel.

You will feel better! No one can make kids stop teasing. But you can talk about your feelings, and that always helps.

Do not tease others.

You are a lot less likely to be teased if you do not tease.

Remember:

You cannot control the kids who tease you.
But you can control what you do when
they tease you.

Read what these kids say about being teased:

"When all my crayons got stolen, I just went to the kid and got them back!"

— *Rex, 8*

"If the kids on the playground keep on following me, I just tell the teacher or ignore them."

— *Stacy, 11*

"When other kids make fun of me, I want to slug them, but I try to ignore them."

— *Reiko, 11*

"I talk to my teacher when kids make me mad. She helps me figure out what some of the kids really said."

— *R.J., 11*

Chapter 10:

Tips For Making
And Keeping Friends

Having friends makes school more fun. But it is not always easy to make friends. Going to LD classes can make it even harder. But this does not mean you cannot do it! Kids with LD can have friends, just like everyone else.

Gary says: "When I think about the kids with LD I have known, I always remember Kenny. Kenny was good at making and keeping friends.

"Kenny was nine when I tested him and found out he had LD. He already had a lot of friends in his regular classroom. He was a friendly boy who helped others and did not tease others. At first he did not want to go to the resource room for help. But his mom and dad said he had to go.

"When Kenny started going to the resource room, he made new friends. But he also kept his old friends. He stayed in LD classes all through grade school and high school. And he always had a lot of friends. Kenny had a talent for making and keeping friends."

The "Making Friends Rules"

Kenny also knew about the "making friends rules." These are different from other kinds of rules.

You do not find them written down in books. You do not find them on signs. You learn them from other people. You learn them from things that happen in your life. Some of them, you learn by making mistakes.

*Read what these kids say about the
"making friends rules":*

"I learned the hard way not to push kids down at
the bus stop. I got pushed down myself."

— *Karla, 9*

"You should respect yourself and respect other kids."

— *Danny, 9*

"You should be nice and gentle with other
people's belongings."

— *Amani, 8*

Some kids with LD have trouble learning the "making friends rules," just like they have trouble learning to read, spell, or do math.

Ways To Make All Kinds Of Friends

Think about the friends you have. Are they all kids who go to LD classes? It is good to have friends who have LD. But it is better to have friends who have LD, AND friends who do not have LD. Like Kenny, you can have both kinds of friends!

What is the best way to make and keep friends? By being a friendly person. Here are some tips to help you be a friendly person.

10 TIPS FOR MAKING AND KEEPING FRIENDS

1. Watch other kids in class and on the playground. See if you can find some who play without teasing or fighting. They would probably make good friends.

2. Take part in games on the playground where kids line up to play and take turns.

3. Watch to see what the other kids like. Find out as much as you can about what they like. Then you can talk with them about the things they like.

4. Do not try to *make* other kids be your friends, especially the most popular ones. You might find good friends in students who are not part of the "in crowd." Is there someone who seems shy? Maybe that person is waiting for *you* to act friendly first.

5. Do not wander around the playground by yourself and hope someone will ask you to play. Instead, choose a game and ask someone to join you.

6. When you play with others, say nice things to them, take your turn, and be a good sport.

7. Do not show off or get into trouble to get noticed.

8. Most people like to talk about themselves. Ask other kids questions about what they like to do. Or ask them about their favorite TV shows, sports, or games.

9. Be friendly, share things, and do not tease. Treat other kids the way you want them to treat you. (That's right: This is the Golden Rule!)

10. Like yourself. Kids like other kids who like themselves.

Chapter 11:

Eight Ways To Get Along At Home

By now you know that you are not stupid. You know you are doing your best work. But maybe other people do not know you are doing your best work. Like your parents.

Maybe your parents have told you, "We know you can do as well as the other kids IF YOU WORK HARD." Maybe they are not the only ones who think this. Sometimes teachers will say things like this to parents of kids with LD:

- "Your child would do fine if he was not so lazy." OR...
- "Your child is smart enough. She just does not pay attention in class." OR...
- "Your child could do good work if he cared more and acted up less."

Then the parents tell the kids, "You are lazy." Or, "You do not pay attention in class." Or, "You do not care about school. You act up too much."

When this happens, kids get upset. If it happens to you, *you* probably get upset. No matter how hard you try in school, you still have a hard time at home!

Maybe it starts right after school. As soon as you get home, your mom or dad meets you at the door. They want you to do your homework RIGHT NOW! It seems like they *never* let up on you.

Summers are not any better. Most kids get to do what they want all summer. They do not even have to think about school for THREE WHOLE MONTHS. Not you, though. You have to go to summer school!

Read what these kids say about their parents:

"Mom cares about me. She tries to help. My dad doesn't understand my problem. It makes me nervous. He thinks I can really hear."

— *Jesse, 11*

"My mom and dad feel good that I'm learning. But they want me to learn better. Sometimes they get mad at me when I don't understand what they want."

— *John, 11*

"I am myself around my parents and if they're mad I listen to them usually, but sometimes I just ignore them."

— *Stacy, 12*

Why do your parents push you to do better all the time? They know you are not stupid. They want you to be the best you can be. They think that if you work harder, you will do better.

Parents do not always understand that kids DO work hard at school. They do not know that kids need time to RELAX.

Maybe you and your parents get upset with each other. They yell at you. You yell back. What follows is one big fight.

But fighting does not help. Talking is better. And talking about your feelings is best. Try telling your parents how you feel. Tell them how hard you work at school. Tell them you do not want to have a hard time at home.

Easy to say, right? Not so easy to do. It is hard to talk out loud about your feelings. Many kids with LD have the same problems with their parents.

Here are some ideas to share with your parents. They are all ways to make things better at home. If you just cannot talk to your parents, maybe you can show them these ideas.

1. Tell Your Parents You Need Time To Relax

Most parents go to work. When they come home from work, do they keep doing that same work? No. To work at the same job 16 hours a day is not fun.

Going to school is your work. If you have to do homework all night, too, that is like working all the time.

This does not mean that you should never do homework. It means that you should also have time to relax. And you should do more relaxing at home than working.

2. Tell Your Parents If Your Homework Takes Too Long

Homework may be good practice for you. And your parents probably think homework is important. Maybe they make sure you do your homework every night.

But do you feel that you are spending ALL of your time doing homework with NO time left over? Then your homework takes too long. To find out why, ask yourself these questions:

- Is it hard to understand what you are supposed to do?
- Is it hard for you to write neatly?
- Is it hard to keep the numbers lined up for math?
- Are you tired from doing schoolwork all day?

Did you answer YES to any of these questions? Then tell your parents or teachers. Or ask your parents to talk to your teachers. Your parents should tell them how long it takes for you to do your homework.

You need time for yourself, too. Ask your parents and teachers if you can work out a plan. The plan should let you do homework and still have time left just for you.

Rhoda says: "When my son, Carter, was in the seventh grade, he brought home 50 or 100 math problems every night. Carter and I would often work on the problems until bedtime. But still he would not get them all done.

"Soon we both were upset. Sometimes we even yelled at each other.

"Finally I called Carter's math teacher. I told her what was happening. I asked the teacher to give Carter fewer math problems for homework.

"I also decided that it was Carter's job to finish his homework. It was not my job to make sure he did. From now on, I said, Carter would be in charge of his own homework.

"The next day, Carter came home again with 50 math problems. He worked on them for a while. Then he stopped to spend some time doing what he wanted to do.

"From then on until he finished high school, Carter was in charge of his own homework. He didn't always make the best grades. But he was happier. And so was I."

3. Tell Your Parents Good News About You

Sometimes parents are asked to come to school to hear about problems. Maybe their children are not doing their school work. Maybe they are acting up. Maybe they are talking back to the teacher.

It is hard for parents to hear bad news. Some parents hear a lot more bad news than good news.

Tell your parents good news about you. Tell them the things you do right each day. Tell them when you are getting better at your school work. Or when the teacher says something nice to you. Or when you make a new friend.

What if your parents are asked to come to school? They can ask to hear good things about you, not just problems. They can tell the people at the school good things about you. Maybe your teachers think you are lazy or not trying. Maybe they do not understand you. Your parents can help. They can tell your teachers what you are really like.

4. Take Time Out When You Need It

Sometimes you may feel so upset that you just want to scream. Or run away and hide.

When you feel that way, take time out. Go for a walk. Go to your room, close the door, and listen to music. Ride your bike. Go fishing.

Do something you like to do. Do NOT do school work.

5. Make A Plan For Your Time

One way to get things done is to make a plan for your time.

Do you have trouble remembering what school work you should do at home? Make a list of the things you are supposed to do at home. Write on your list everything you need to bring home. Bring the list home, too. Make a check by each thing on your list after you do it.

Decide what time you will do your school work. Right after you get home? After dinner? Pick a time when someone is there to help you if you need help.

Before you start your schoolwork, find everything you need. Pencils, books, papers? What else? Turn off the TV and the radio. Do not call up friends on the telephone. Perhaps you can even put a DO NOT DISTURB sign at your table. Then WORK!

6. Eat Well

Did you know that "junk foods" like pop, chips, and candy make it hard to think? Healthy foods like fruits and vegetables can help you think better.

If you need a snack, eat the good stuff. Skip the junk food. Do your brain a favor!

7. Find A Hobby

Find something you like to do that gets your mind off school. Keep a pet. Collect rocks. Learn to use a computer.

Finding a hobby will also give you something to share with others. You may even become an expert.

Remember that being an expert is a good way to show that people with LD can be smart. It is also a good way to get attention.

8. Get A Job

Get a paper route. Babysit. Cut the neighbor's lawn. Collect and sell cans.

Getting a job will help keep your mind off school. It will help you think about what you want to do when you get out of school. You will also make some money.

On page 91 of this book, there is a part called "Home and Homework." It tells about some of the things in this chapter. Show this note to your parents. It can help them understand why you need time away from school work. And why home should be a place to relax.

Chapter 12:

What Happens When You Grow Up?

Right now you might think, "I will *never* get out of school!" But you will be out of school and grown up before you know it. Maybe you think that once you are out of school, all your problems will be over. No more teachers on your back. No more nagging from your parents. You will be on your own. You can do what you want!

That is not the way it is. Being an adult is not easy. Doing just what you want can get you into trouble. When you become an adult, you must take care of yourself. There are lots of things adults must do that you may not be thinking about. It is important to know these things if you want to become independent.

We will tell you some things adults must do. We will also tell you some things you can do to get ready to be an adult. There are many things you can do right now. There are others you can do when you are old enough.

An Adult Can Find A Job

Right now, you can:

- Find out about different kinds of work by asking people about their jobs.
- Practice filling out job applications.
- Learn to read the newspaper ads.
- Talk to a job counselor about how to get a job.
- Practice looking for work with a parent, teacher or an adult you know who owns a business.
- Do volunteer work.

When you are old enough, you can:
- Find a job of your own.
- Be a good worker. To be a good worker, you must:
  — Do what you say you will do.
  — Always be on time for work.
  — Accept helpful suggestions from other people.
  — Admit it when you make a mistake. Do not blame your mistakes on someone or something else.

An Adult Can Keep House

Right now, you can:
- Help with the work at home. You can:
  — Scrub the bathroom.
  — Vacuum or mop the floors.
  — Dust the furniture.
  — Mow the lawn.
  — Water the plants.
- Keep your own room neat and clean.

An Adult Can Manage Money

Right now, you can:
- Ask your parents for an allowance so you can learn to manage money.

- Pay for some of your own clothes, movies, and other things you want.
- Save some of your money in the bank.
- Open a bank account and learn how to write checks.
- Start planning ways you may need money in the future. Will you go to college? Will you want a car?

An Adult Can Eat Right

Right now, you can:
- Plan a meal.
- Make a shopping list.
- Buy groceries, including plenty of healthful foods such as fruits and vegetables.
- Learn to cook. You could even have a meal ready for your parents when they come home from work.
- Stay away from junk foods like candy, chips, and pop. They cost a lot and are not good for you.

An Adult Can Look Good

Right now, you can:
- Take a bath or shower every day.
- Get a haircut when you need one.
- Learn to wash your own clothes.
- Brush your teeth, wash up often, and use deodorant if you need it.

An Adult Can Get Around Town

Right now, you can:
- Learn to use a bus or taxi.
- Learn how to read maps.

When you are old enough, you can:
- Take driver's ed in school.
- Get a driver's license.
- Learn how to take care of a car.
- Learn how to get a car license and car insurance.

An Adult Can Make Friends

Right now, you can:

- Form a support group with other people who have LD. Ask your parents for help getting started. Or ask the resource room or LD teacher at your school.

A support group is a group of people who have something in common. They have meetings where they talk and make friends. A support group is a safe place to talk about problems or things you are worried about. It is also a good place to have fun.

- Join clubs that do things you enjoy, like bird watching, bicycling, or hiking.
- Go to a church or temple.
- Be a volunteer. Work in a hospital or nursing home. Take hot meals to older people.

An Adult Can Get Married

Right now, you can:

- Ask your parents and other adults you like and trust to tell you about marriage.
- Practice sharing with others.

An Adult Can Raise A Family

Right now, you can:

- Do volunteer work in a child care center.
- Babysit.
- Ask your parents what it is like to have children. Have them tell you about the problems as well as the good things.

Remember:

Being an adult is not easy. Becoming independent takes a lot of time, thought, and work. It is never too early to learn the skills you will need after you are out of school.

A Happy Ending: You Can Be A Winner!

We'd like to tell you about two people we know. Ana and Bill are adults who have LD.

Ana's Story

Ana has finished six years of college. Now she is a school counselor. She still has a hard time with spelling, and she reads slowly.

All through school, Ana had to study very hard. But she is very bright. She is also a very friendly person. Ana is a person with LD, and she's a winner.

Bill's Story

Bill went to LD classes all through high school. He finished high school, but he didn't want to go to college. He wanted to fix cars.

Bill got a job as a helper at a car repair shop. He always went to work on time, worked hard, and was polite. Bill also tried to learn everything he could about fixing cars. He asked questions and watched carefully.

Soon Bill got promoted to car mechanic. He did so well that he was made the supervisor of the shop. He still has a hard time reading and must ask for help sometimes. Bill is a person with LD, and he's a winner.

You can be a winner, too. There is no magic cure for LD. There is no pill, way of teaching, or diet that can make you not have LD. But having LD does not stop a person from doing great things and being happy and successful.

Now that you have read this book, you know there are ways to make things better at school and at home. Use these suggestions and remember:

You are a person with LD.

You are also a great kid.

You are a WINNER!

Ten More Things You Might Want To Know About LD

When kids find out they have LD, they want to know more about it. Here are 10 questions kids have asked us about LD.

If your parents and teachers want to know more about LD, you can show them these pages.

1. Is Dyslexia The Same Thing As LD?

No. Dyslexia (dis LEK sē ə) is a kind of LD in which a person has a lot of trouble with reading. But not all people with reading problems have dyslexia.

Only about one to three percent of people with reading problems have dyslexia. The others cannot read well because of other problems. These problems might be:

- they have trouble sitting still,
- they do not have enough interest in reading, or
- they are not paying attention.

Some people with LD can read well, but they have trouble in other areas such as math, language (talking and listening), or making friends.

2. Does Having LD Mean That I Have Brain Damage?

This is a good question. Even the experts have trouble answering it.

About 100 years ago, some doctors saw that some smart kids had trouble learning. Those kids were like people who had strokes, a disease that causes brain damage. Both kinds of people can have problems with language (talking and listening), planning things, and moving their bodies.

Years later, some other doctors saw that kids with LD were like soldiers with head injuries. Both kinds of people had many of the same problems, like problems with language (talking and listening). So, many doctors today do think that kids with LD may have brain damage.

But other doctors do not agree. They think kids with LD have problems because they started school too early. Or they did not get enough help, or the right kind of help, from parents or teachers.

Perhaps a few kids with LD do have brain damage. But no one knows for sure.

3. Does LD Ever Go Away?

This is a hard question. The answer depends on many things, like:

- How many ways does the person have LD? Only in one way, like reading? Or in many ways?
- How early did parents and teachers find out about the LD? Since then, what kind of help has the person with LD been given?
- How helpful has the person's school been? Do the teachers, principal, and psychologist know about LD? Have they tried to learn more about it and understand it better?
- How helpful have the person's parents been? How much do they know about LD?
- How independent has the person with LD been allowed to be?

And, if the person with LD is an adult,

- What kind of work does the person with LD do? Has he or she had good work experiences? Did the person have help finding and choosing a job after school was over?

While LD may not go away, most people with LD can do many things if they have the right help. This help must begin very early in their lives.

4. Can I Go To College If I Have LD?

This is a hard question, too. It depends on what kind of help you get, and how hard it is for you to do school work. It depends on how much you want to go to college, and how important college is to get the job you want.

You need to finish college to get only about nine percent of the jobs in this country. Some people with LD do finish college. Many others have a hard time with it and never finish.

We do not think that going to college is something you have to do. Going to college does not mean that a person will be happy and successful as an adult. But if you want to go to college, you should try. Ask your parents and teachers what they think. Ask them to help you try.

Think about what kind of college you might want to go to. There are four-year colleges, two-year colleges, and junior colleges.

There are colleges you can go to in the evenings so you can have a job at the same time. These schools are not as big or confusing as the four-year colleges, and you could take other kinds of classes at the same time. When you finish there, you can decide if you want to go to college some more.

▶ If you go to a four-year college, choose one that has special programs for people with LD. Many colleges do. For help in finding these colleges, write to:

LDA
4156 Library Road
Pittsburgh, PA 15234

National Center for Learning Disabilities Inc.(NCLD)
99 Park Avenue
New York, NY 10016

Ask them to send you information about colleges for people with LD.

▶ Find out more about colleges by writing to:

American Council on Education
One Dupont Circle NW, Suite 800
Washington, DC 20036-1193

Ask them to send you their paper called "Learning Disabled Adults in Postsecondary Education." They will send you one copy for free.

▶ Here is a book that you can check out from the library:

Peterson's Guide to Colleges with Programs for Learning Disabled Students, Charles T. Mangrum II, Ed. D. and Stephen S. Strichert, Ph. D., Editors (Princeton, NJ: Petersons Guides 1988).

If you do not want to go to college, you can make other plans. Go to vocational school. Become a hairdresser or a mechanic, an animal-doctor's helper, a computer repair-person. Try to think about what you are good at. Then get some training in that area.

▶ Here are some books that can help you make plans without college:

Guide to Alternative Education and Training by Vivian Dubrovin (New York: Franklin Watts, 1988).

Guide to Careers Without College by Kathleen S. Abrams. (New York: Franklin Watts, 1988).

5. If I Have Children, Will They Have LD?

No one knows for sure. It is true that some families have many people with LD. Not just brothers and sisters, but cousins and nieces and uncles as well.

We do not know why these families have many people with LD. Did they inherit it? Or did they get it because they have the same background and many of the same experiences?

▼ ━━━━━━━━━━━━━━━━━━━━━━━ ▼

Inherit (in HER it)
means "to get it from your parents or grandparents."

▲ ━━━━━━━━━━━━━━━━━━━━━━━ ▲

80

If you decide to have children of your own, talk to a doctor or an LD teacher. They can tell you more about your chances of having kids with LD.

Many people with LD have children who do have LD. Many people with LD have children who do not have LD. Here is what you need to think about: Could you love and take care of a child, no matter what? That is the most important thing to decide.

6. Will I Be Able To Work And Live On My Own Someday?

Most people with LD can become as independent as other people. It just may take more planning and work. That's why we think you should start to prepare for your future right now.

Start thinking about all you will need to do to be a good worker and live on your own. Get practice by working as soon as you can. You can get a paper route, work on a ranch, or get a job in a fast-food restaurant.

The earlier you learn about work, the more likely you will learn the skills you need to be a good worker.

We also think it is important for you to learn to make your own decisions. Practice being independent as soon as you can. Make choices about the clothes you wear. Finish your school work on your own. Help with work around the house. There are many things you can do!

7. Do All Kids With LD Read And Write Words Backwards?

No. Only a very few kids with LD have this problem. It is called "mirror writing." Everything they see looks the way it would look in a mirror.

Many young children ages seven and eight see letters and words backwards when they are first learning to read and write. This is not a problem unless it keeps up as the children grow older.

If you have this problem, go and see a psychologist who works with people with LD. Ask your school psychologist, counselor, or social worker for the names of some psychologists. Then tell your parents the names.

Many times, kids who have this problem can be helped to get over it. Then they do not read and write words backwards anymore.

8. Are All Kids With LD Alike?

NO! Kids with LD can be very different from each other. (Just like other kids.) But there is one way they are alike: It is hard for them to learn. That is why they are in the same LD classes at school.

9. Are There More Boys Or Girls With LD?

Three out of every four kids with LD are boys. No one knows why. Maybe boys are more likely to inherit LD (get it from their parents or grandparents). We do know that more boys inherit health problems than girls do.

Also, boys are often more active than girls. Sometimes it is harder for them to sit still in school. They may act up more and seem less interested in doing school work. Teachers and parents might think they have LD when they really do not.

10. Should All Kids With LD Be Put In Regular Classes?

No. Public Law 94-142 says that kids should be taught in the right kind of classes to help them learn. Some kids with LD do fine in a regular classroom. Others learn best in an LD classroom.

LD classes are often better for learning. They are smaller, quieter, and less confusing. Plus the LD teacher knows how to teach in ways that help LD kids to learn.

Special Section:

For Parents And Teachers

In this section you will find suggestions for teaching and learning materials which are helpful for kids with LD, information about depression (a common problem among kids with LD), ways to handle homework, and a bibliography, should you wish to read more about LD.

We welcome your comments, ideas, and recommendations. Please feel free to write to us:

Gary Fisher and Rhoda Cummings
c/o Free Spirit Publishing
400 First Avenue North, Suite 616
Minneapolis, MN 55401

Learning Resources for Kids with LD

Records and Audio Cassettes

The Survival Guide For Kids With LD is available on audio cassette. See page 97 for details.

Children who have difficulty reading can benefit from books on tape (or record). For information and lists of available books, write:

Recording for the Blind, Inc.
20 Roszel Road
Princeton, NJ 08540
Telephone: (609) 452-0606

National Library Services for the Blind
 and Physically Handicapped
1291 Taylor Street NW
Washington, DC 20452
Telephone: (202) 707-5100

When writing the National Library Services, request information about "Talking Books" from the Library of Congress.

Books

Check your local library, order through your favorite bookstore, or write to the publisher at the address provided.

Male, Mary. *Special Magic: Computers, Classroom Strategies, and Exceptional Children* (Mountain View, CA: Mayfield Publishing Co., 1988). Address: 1240 Villa St., Mountain View, California 94041.

Kreivsky, Joseph and Linfield, Jordan. *The Bad Speller's Dictionary* (New York: Random House, 1974). Address: Random House, Inc., 201 East 50th St., New York, NY 10022.

Kits

Survival Skills: Activity Card Kits, Study Skills: Activity Binder, and the *Hi/Lo Reading Series* are high interest/low reading level books and activity cards for children with LD in grades 4–12. For more information, write:

Sunburst Communications
101 Castleton Ave.
Pleasantville, NY 10570-9971
Or call toll-free (800) 431-1934

Computer Software

Check your local library first; many libraries now carry computer software and are equipped with computers so you can try before you buy. Or write to the addresses shown below. When available, catalog numbers are listed for your convenience.

For our numbers 1–5, write:

Cambridge Development Laboratory, Inc.,
Dept. NUMEROBIN
214 – 3rd Avenue
Waltham, MA 02154
Or call toll-free (800) 637-0047
In Massachusetts call (617) 890-4640

You may want to request their catalog, *Special Times: Special Education Software for Grades K–8.*

1. "101 Misused Words: Grades 4–8" (The Learning Seed Company). Cat. #3-LEL-03A (Apple); Cat. #3-LEL-03I (IBM). Program offers 500 practice sentences to teach correct use of 50 commonly confused word pairs such as "accept/except" and "to/two/too." Also includes a definition and explanation of each word.

2. "Where in the World is Carmen Sandiego?" (Broderbund Software). Cat. #4-BDL-O5A (Apple); Cat. #4-BDL-05I (IBM). Students explore great cities of the world in hot pursuit of master thieves who have stolen the Statue of Liberty's torch. Students learn to read for meaning and gain understanding of world geography. Appropriate for individual and group instruction in classroom and resource room.

3. "The Calendar: Grades 2–8" (Gamco Software). Cat. #7-GAM-05A (Apple). Lets students combine practice in calendar skills with an arcade game. Also includes a teacher management system to integrate learning from other curriculum areas by customizing content of questions and calendar-related information.

4. "Money Management" (Marshware). Cat. #3-MAM-02A (Apple). Grades 4–12. Assists students in planning and controlling personal finances. Students with LD at an intermediate level can learn about credit cards, loans, and mortgages. Includes on-line calculator.

5. "Clock: Grades 1–5" (Heartsoft). Cat. #4-HTM-07A (Apple). Grades 1–4. Simple, easy-to-use program for children who are learning how to read time of day from clocks and digital displays. Teacher management system records student performance.

For our numbers 6–7, write:

Scholastic Inc.
2931 East McCarty St.
Jefferson City, MO 65102
Or call toll-free (800) 541-5513

6. "Bankstreet Writer III." Simple-to-learn word processor for Apple or IBM.

7. "Talking Text Writer." A word processor that reads back every letter, word, or sentence in a clear voice.

For our number 8, write:

Sunburst Communications
101 Castleton Ave.
Pleasantville, NY 10570-9971
Or call toll-free (800) 431-1934

8. "Magic Slate II." Simple-to-learn word processor for Grades 2–adult. The 20-column version features large letters and simplified commands.

Help for Kids with Depression

Children who are depressed may exhibit a wide variety of symptoms, making diagnosis difficult. Like depressed adults, children may cry easily and frequently, have sleeping and eating problems, and be tired or sick a great deal. Unlike adults, depressed children are sometimes sullen, hostile, and aggressive. They throw tantrums over small issues or strike out at others in reaction to insignificant events.

Obviously, all children demonstrate some of the above symptoms at various times. However, kids with LD are more likely to become depressed than other children due to their difficulty in understanding their condition and the frustrations they encounter.

In most schools, a school counselor, psychologist, or social worker will be available to guide you to the most appropriate place to receive assistance if you believe your child is depressed. In some communities, you may need to contact a community mental health center or your family physician for diagnostic assistance and referrals.

There are materials available to assist children in self-understanding and to promote a positive self-concept. Such materials may facilitate your child's expression of his or her feelings.

Following are suggestions based on our experience working with children with LD. Parents, we recommend that you consult with your child's teacher and school counselor, psychologist, or social worker before choosing any materials to try at home. Teachers, please talk to the parents, as well as the school counselor, psychologist, or social worker.

Books

Canfield, J., and Wells, H.C. *100 Ways To Enhance Self-Concept in the Classroom: A Handbook for Teachers and Parents* (Englewood Cliffs, NJ: Prentice-Hall, 1976).

Freed, A.M., *TA for Teens (And Other Important People)* (Los Angeles: Jalmar Press, 1976).

Hendricks, G. and Wills, R. *The Centering Book: Awareness Activities for Children, Parents and Teachers* (Englewood Cliffs, NJ: Prentice-Hall, 1975).

Hendricks, G. and Roberts, T.B. *The Second Centering Book: More Awareness Activities for Children, Parents and Teachers* (Englewood Cliffs, NJ: Prentice-Hall, 1977).

Kaufman, G. and Raphael, L. *Stick Up For Yourself! Every Kid's Guide to Personal Power and Positive Self-Esteem* (Minneapolis, MN: Free Spirit Publishing, 1990).

Marek, M. *Different, Not Dumb* (New York: Franklin Watts, 1986).

Magazine

Their World. Published once a year, this magazine contains articles, drawings, and photographs from parents, children, and professionals concerning their experiences with learning disabilities. It is primarily for adults but has some items of interest to kids. For subscription information, write:

National Center for Learning Disabilities Inc. (NCLD)
99 Park Avenue
New York, NY 10016
Or call (212) 687-7211

Film

"Learning Disabilities — First Hand." This 15-minute film discusses the academic and emotional obstacles for persons with learning disabilities. For more information, write:

Lawren Productions
930 Pitner Avenue
Evanston, IL 60202
Or call toll-free (800) 323-9084

Organizations

The following organizations provide information and/or support for kids or adults with LD and their families.

Learning Disabilities Association (LDA)
4156 Library Road
Pittsburgh, PA 15234
Telephone: (412) 341-1515

Membership includes professionals and parents devoted to advancing the education and well-being of children and adults with learning disabilities. Publishes a newsletter six times per year and holds an annual international conference. Contact the national organization for information on state and local chapters.

Association of Learning Disabled Adults
PO Box 9722
Friendship Station
Washington, DC 20016
Telephone: (301) 593-1035

A self-help group for adults with learning disabilities. Will provide assistance to those who wish to organize self-help groups.

CHADD
Children with Attention Deficit Disorder
300 NW 70th Ave., Suite 102
Plantation, FL 33317
Telephone: (305) 792-8100 or (305) 384-6869

This organization provides resources and support for parents of children who suffer from attention deficit disorder.

Council for Exceptional Children (CEC)
1920 Association Drive
Reston, VA 22091
Telephone: (703) 620-3660

The Council for Exceptional Children (CEC) is the only professional organization in the world dedicated to advancing the quality of education for all exceptional children and improving the conditions under which special educators work.

National Center for Learning Disabilities Inc. (NCLD)
99 Park Avenue
New York, NY 10016
Telephone: (212) 687-7211

Formerly the Foundation for Children with Learning Disabilities. Promotes public awareness about learning disabilities, neurological disorders, and deficits which can be a barrier to literacy. Provides resources and referrals on a national level to a wide range of volunteers and professionals.

Marin Puzzle People, Inc.
17 Buena Vista Ave.
Mill Valley, CA 94941
Telephone: (415) 383-8763

An organization of adults with learning disabilities. Offers social functions, minicourses, information, and referral services. Publishes a monthly newsletter and a booklet to assist those who wish to start local clubs.

National Network of Learning Disabled Adults
808 N. 82nd Street, Suite F2
Scottsdale, AZ 85257
Telephone: (602) 941-5112

This organization is run by people with learning disabilities. Provides assistance to those who wish to develop self-help groups for adults with LD. Publishes a newsletter and list of self-help groups.

Orton Dyslexia Society
724 York Road
Baltimore, MD 21204
Telephone: (301) 296-0232

This is a scientific and educational association which does have parents as members. The concern of the society is developmental dyslexia. State chapters hold at least one public meeting or workshop per year. The society publishes books, packets, and reprints pertaining to dyslexia.

Home and Homework

All of us who are parents want to be good parents. We think that one way to do this is to make sure our kids do their homework.

There is nothing wrong with this way of thinking, at least where most kids are concerned. However, if your child has learning disabilities, you might want to be more careful not to pressure your child too much about homework.

Because our children have learning problems, we sometimes think that we can "make them" improve by hiring a tutor, or seeing to it that they do their homework every night, or enrolling them in summer school. While all of this emphasis on school may improve our kids' academics, we hate to think of what it is doing to their emotional well-being!

For most kids with LD, school is tough. It is tough all day, every day. Try to imagine what it is like to be frustrated all day long, and then come home and be forced to do *more* school work until bedtime.

We believe that home should be a haven for children with learning disabilities. Home should be a place for them to relax. It should be a place where they can be themselves. If teachers are assigning too much homework, we suggest that you speak to those teachers. Ask them if they can assign less work. Why assign 50 math problems if the student can work 5–10 correctly? You might also remind teachers that an assignment that takes most kids 15 minutes to complete will take a learning disabled child at least an hour to finish.

Bibliography: For Further Reading

Cummings, R. and Maddux, C. *Parenting the Learning Disabled: A Realistic Approach* (Springfield, IL: Charles C. Thomas, 1985).

Cummings, R. and Maddux, C. *Career and Vocational Education for the Mildly Handicapped* (Springfield, IL: Charles C. Thomas, 1987).

Kirk, S.A. and Chalfant, J.C. *Academic and Developmental Learning Disabilities* (Denver: Love Publishing Co., 1984).

Kronick, D. *Social Development of Learning Disabled Persons* (San Francisco: Jossey-Bass, 1981).

Lerner, J. *Learning Disabilities: Theories, Diagnosis, and Teaching Strategies* (Boston: Houghton Mifflin Co., 1988).

Smith, S. *No Easy Answers: The Learning Disabled Child* (New York: Bantam Books, 1981).

Index

A

Academic and Developmental Learning Disabilities, 92
Academic learning disability, 17
Adulthood, 71–76, 79–81
American Council on Education, 80
Anger, 39–44, 48, 51–52
Association of Learning Disabled Adults, 89
Attention deficit disorder, 18–19
Attentiveness, 18–19

B

Bad Speller's Dictionary, The, 85
Bancroft, Ann, 45
Brain:
 damage, 77–78
 messages from ears and eyes, 11–14

C

Cambridge Development Laboratory, 86
Career and Vocational Education for the Mildly Handicapped, 92
CEC, 90
Centering Book: Awareness Activities for Children, Parents and Teachers, The, 88
CHADD, 89
Children with Attention Deficit Disorder (CHADD), 89
Classrooms for kids with LD, 24–33, 82
College, 79–80
Communication skills, 39–44, 48
Computer software, 86–87
Council for Exceptional Children (CEC), 90
Counselor, 42

D

Depression, 41–44, 87–89
Diet, 69, 73
Different, Not Dumb, 88
Dyslexia, 77, 91

E

Ears, how they work, 11–12
Edison, Thomas, 45
Education for All
 Handicapped Children
 Act, 25–26, 29–30, 82
Einstein, Albert, 45
Emotionally disturbed kids,
 29
Excuses, using LD, 52
Eyes, how they work, 12–14

F

Famous people with LD, 45
Feelings, 39–45, 48, 87–89
Feelings LD, 20–21
Foundation for Children
 with Learning
 Disabilities. *See*
 National Center for
 Learning Disabilities
 (NCLD)
Friendships, 50, 59–61

G

Getting along at home,
 63–69
Getting along in school,
 47–52
*Guide to Alternative
 Education and Training*,
 80
*Guide to Careers Without
 College*, 80

H

Hampshire, Susan, 45
High interest/low reading
 level resources, 86

Hobbies, 49, 69
Home life, 63–69
Homework, 65–68, 85
Household chores, 72
How to handle being
 teased, 55–58
Hurt feelings, 39–44, 48

I

IEP (Individualized
 Education Program),
 32–33
Independence, 37–38,
 71–74, 81
Inheriting LD, chances of,
 80–81

J

Jenner, Bruce, 45
Jobs, 69, 71–72

L

Language learning disability, 18
Lawren Productions, 89
LD:
 definition of, 2–4, 30
 kinds of, 17–21
 programs for, 31–33
 questions about, 77–82
 reasons for, 8–9
 well-known people with,
 45
LDA, 23, 29, 79, 89
Learning different, definition of, 2–4. *See also* LD
Learning Disabilities
 Association (LDA), 23,
 29, 79, 89

Learning disabled:
  definition of, 4, 30
  types of, 17–21
  See also LD
"Learning
    Disabilities—First
    Hand," 89
Learning Disabilities:
    Theories, Diagnosis, and
    Teaching Strategies, 92
Learning resources, 85–87
Learning styles, 14–16
Louganis, Greg, 45

M

Mainstreaming, 26–27
Making friends, 50, 59–61,
  74
Marin Puzzle People, 90
Money management,
  72–73
Motor disability, 20
Moving LD, 20

N

National Center for
  Learning Disabilities
  (NCLD), 79, 88
National Library Services
  for the Blind and
  Physically
  Handicapped, 85
National Network of
  Learning Disabled
  Adults, 90–91
No Easy Answers: The
  Learning Disabled Child,
  92
Nutrition, 69, 73

O

100 Ways to Enhance Self-
  Concept in the
  Classroom: A
  Handbook for Teachers
  and Parents, 88
Organizations, 89–91
Orton Dyslexia Society, 90

P

Parent resources, 85–92
Parenting the Learning
    Disabled: A Realistic
    Approach, 92
Parents, LD kids and, 23,
  63–69
Paying attention LD, 18–19
Perceptual motor disability,
  20
Peterson's Guide to Colleges
    with Programs for
    Learning Disabled
    Students, 80
Physically or sensory
  handicapped kids, 30
Planning time, 67–68
Psychologist, 25, 31, 82
Public Law 94-142, 26,
  29–30, 82

R

Recording for the Blind, 85
Records and audio cas-
  settes, 85
Relaxation, 64–65
Resource materials, 85–87,
  92
Resource room, 26-27

Retarded kids:
  definition of, 24, 30
  differences from LD kids,
    23–24, 35–38
Rockefeller, Nelson, 45

S

Sadness, 39–44, 48
Scholastic Inc., 87
School:
  getting along better,
    47–52
  handling teasers, 53–58
  participating in activities,
    50
School work LD, 17
*Second Centering Book: More
  Awareness Activities for
  Children, Parents and
  Teachers, The*, 88
Self-help groups, 89–91
*Social Development of
  Learning Disabled
  Persons*, 92
Social perceptual disability,
  20–21
Social skills deficit, 20–21
*Special Magic: Computers,
  Classroom Strategies,
  and Exceptional Students*,
  85
Special needs students,
  25–30
*Stick Up for Yourself! Every
  Kid's Guide to Personal
  Power and Positive Self-
  Esteem*, 88
Stress, 51–52, 55–57

Success, 71–76
Sunburst Communications,
  86

T

*TA for Teens (And Other
  Important People)*, 88
"Talking Books," 85
Talking and listening LD,
  18
Teacher resources, 85–92
Teasing, 53–58
Testing for LD, 9, 25, 31–33
Their World (magazine), 88

V

Vocational preparation,
  79–80

W

Ways to get along better in
  school, 47–52
Ways to help depression,
  42–45
Ways to learn, 14–16
Ways to make friends,
  59–61, 74
Well-known persons with
  LD, 45
Wilson, Woodrow, 45

The Survival Guide for Kids with LD complete text is available on audio cassette. If you would like to order the audio cassette version of this book, write or call for our free catalog. Our address and phone number are listed below.

Other Free Spirit materials you will find helpful...

SCHOOL POWER
Strategies for Succeeding in School
by Jeanne Shay Schumm and Marguerite Radencich

THE SCHOOL SURVIVAL GUIDE
FOR KIDS WITH LD*
(*Learning Differences)
by Rhoda Cummings and Gary Fisher

STICK UP FOR YOURSELF!
Every Kid's Guide to Personal Power and Positive Self-Esteem
by Gershen Kaufman and Lev Raphael

FIGHTING INVISIBLE TIGERS:
A Stress Management Guide for Teens
by Earl Hipp

DREAMS CAN HELP:
A Journal Guide to Understanding Your Dreams
and Making Them Work for You
by Jonni Kincher

Free Spirit Publishing Inc.
400 First Avenue North, Suite 616
Minneapolis MN 55401
1 (800) 735-7323